better together*

*This book is best read together, grownup and kid.

akidsbookabout.com

a kids book about^{TM}

a kids book about

DEPRESSION

by Kileah McIlvain

a
kids
book
about™

Printed in the United States of America

Library of Congress cataloging available.

A Kids Book About books are exclusively available online
on the A Kids Book About website.

To share your stories, ask questions, or inquire about bulk
purchases (schools, libraries, and nonprofits), please use
the following email address:

hello@akidsbookabout.com

www.akidsbookabout.com

ISBN: 978-1-951253-04-2

For Micah and our hobbits.

Intro

Hey Grownup, I know that delving into the subject of depression can feel like jumping off the diving board into an ocean of unknowns. I hope you know that your willingness to discuss this topic with your kid opens up a safe space and place of compassion as you navigate these waters together.

Vulnerability is the soil of connection and growth, and it's a privilege to walk with you and your kid as you discuss the topic of depression together. I hope it gives you a framework to better understand yourself, or your child, or a loved one in your life.

Hi, my name is Kileah...
(Ky-LEE-Uh)

and I have depression.

Have you ever heard the word "depression" before?

It might sound new,
strange,
or even scary.

But it's actually something
a lot of people have.

I am one of those people.

Let me share
my story with you.

I don't remember the first time I felt my depression.

I didn't even know that
what I was feeling
had a name.

But it felt like being trapped...

in
a
fog
that
I
couldn't
see
through
clearly.

Talking, laughing, and doing
fun things didn't seem
to matter anymore.

Color even seemed to lose its **Color**.

Songs sounded like noise noise
no
nois
noise
noise
noise
noise
noise
noise
noise
noise
noise
noise
noise
noise
noise
noise
noise
no
no
noise
no
no

noise. noise
noise noise
noise
noise noisnoise
noise noise
noise noise
noise noise noise
noise noise
noise noise
noise
noise
noise
noise
noise
noise
noise
noise
noise
noise
noise
noise
noise
noise
noise
noise
noise
noise
noise
noise
noise
noise
noise
noise
noise
noise noise
noise.
noise
noise noise

And
nothing felt kind,
or beautiful,
or safe.

When I felt depressed, it made me feel lonely and scared.

Like if I felt too much sadness,
I would get swallowed up
in that fog and
disappear

Everything made me
feel like crying or
being angry.

Sometimes for no
reason at all.

And sometimes, I didn't

el

even when I wanted to.

It seemed like anything I did
or said was wrong,
and that I wasn't
ever enough.

The longer this went on...

the more I would feel:

useless

wrong

bad

lonely

scared

invisible.

And of course, I thought I was the only one who felt this way!

But, maybe I *wasn't* the only one.

Have you ever felt this way?

Like... there's a wall separating you from everyone else?

Like... you can't be happy, no matter how hard you try?

Like... you don't get to choose how you feel?

Like... everyone thinks you're fine, but you're not?

That's depression.

Depression is a disorder that causes the brain to feel so sad, discouraged, and lonely that it gets in the way of living everyday life.

So, how did I find out
I had depression?

Well, one day I started to cry, and
I couldn't stop...

And words and tears came
flooding out of me
like an ocean.

And I told the most important
person in my life all of
the things that I had
been feeling inside
of me.

The things that they couldn't see.

I told this person about
the fog,
the sadness,
and the loneliness.

And they **hugged** me...

And they finally saw
what was going
on inside
of me.

Finally...

I WASN'T ALONE ANYMORE!

I didn't know exactly
what I needed,

but I knew that I needed...

So I got help,
and help looked like this:

Meeting with a doctor.

Letting myself feel.

Talking to others.

Giving myself a break.

Trying medicine.

Doing things I loved again.

Not having to be alone.

If you feel like this now
or ever have before,
help may look like:

Telling someone you feel safe with.

Talking with a counselor.

Letting others take care of you.

Helping others in need.

Or trying medicine.

When I got help...

something...

amazing...

started...

happening...

Sharing about my depression took the bricks from the walls built around my heart.

And turned them into a bridge.

A bridge back to me.

The real me.

And I started to notice all
of the color and music
and smiles around
me again.

I could sit in the sunlight
and laugh without
pretending
anymore.

I was learning to see through
the darkness and the fog...

without letting it
take over.

So now, when I start to feel depressed, I...

Remember I'm not alone.

Tell someone how I'm feeling.

Do something that makes me happy.

And **ask** for help.

Outro

Hey Grownup, you might have seen a lot of things in this book that mirror what you see in your own life, or your child's life, or that of a loved one. I can imagine you may have your own questions. The biggest one probably being, "Where do we go from here?"

First, you aren't alone. Let the child you know or person you love know that, too.

Next, ask them how they're feeling, and be open to sharing your own feelings, too. Share that you've noticed that things seem different with them and that you want to be there for them.

After that, ask how you can help, even if they don't know exactly what they need. Do they need someone to listen? Can you help them find a doctor who can help? A group they can join? Above all, be there for them. Listen to them. Be open to how they're feeling.

find more kids books about

belonging, feminism, money, racism, creativity, failure, gratitude, adventure, cancer, body image, and mindfulness.

akidsbookabout.com

notes

share
your read*

*Tell somebody, post a photo, or give this book away to share what you care about.

@akidsbookabout